If Emotions Could Speak

AF624663

Gabrielle Parent

BookLeaf Publishing

Presentation by *BookLeaf Publishing*

Web: www.bookleafpub.com

E-mail: info@bookleafpub.com

ISBN: 978-93-95784-08-5

First edition 2022

DEDICATION

I dedicate these pages to all my teachers throughout my life who believed in my words, continually whispering in my ear: "Just keep writing..."

PREFACE

I have been told I have a way with words, which for the longest time just made me stand there, mouth agape, wondering if they were actually talking to someone else standing behind me. Because I grew up having so little control over my words, knowing so little vocabulary, it mostly didn't come out at all. My younger self felt powerless, and frustrated, seeing how others could literally change the world if you knew how to express yourself properly.

So I started writing, and sharing, initially very clumsily, but slowly learning how to let my emotions do the speaking. In my head emotions have always been quite alive and worth listening to if you knew their language. Somehow, I was learning.

Over the years, I've used writing to give space to those emotions to let me know what is going on inside my brain. Having a peculiar brain that has had its share of mental instability, it is at times solely frustrating and at others very satisfying to let them express themselves on paper.

I live for having someone read one of my poems and think "yeah, me too." It's to shine a light on matters that aren't exactly easy to talk about or to describe but are somehow so very human. Yet, there is still so much stigma toward people with mental health issues.

I hope this brings others comfort, reflection, and maybe just a little bit more insight into what it is to live with mental illnesses.

Sunflowers On The Walls

I want to paint sunflowers on my walls
Yellow, bright, nurturing plants
That always know how to find
The light.

I finally have space to paint
These sunflowers on my walls
Imperfect, messy, spilling
The colors onto my
Makeshift canvas.

There is this heaviness in my chest
As if someone is gripping my heart
From the inside and squeezing
So hard, letting me know
That my soul is aching,
Crying for the ones who
Let the flame burn out.

Over the last few weeks,
I've been calling, caring,
Connecting, reminding some of
My closest humans that they are
Loved and that life is worth living.

We navigated this overburdened
Healthcare system that advertises
That you matter but that they can
Only care after the one year waitlist
Gets to you.

Until then, be patient.
That's simple, right?

So I am painting sunflowers,
To give my heart a break,
To remember that caring also
Involves self-care and that
Self-care, for me, involves
Words and paint and colors
And the chaos of creation.

I am creating flowers out of nothing
And nothing out of such a heavy
Weight pressing down on me.
The more I create, the more my
Heart feels light, freed from the
Emotions that had nowhere to go.

During these times of isolation,
I hope you have your own sunflowers,
Or people who bring some to you
And teaches you how to pick them
Again among the wilderness.

I hope sunflowers bloom throughout
Your street, between neighbours,
Strangers,
A little light among the dark,
A little reminder of how beautiful
Life can be.

Don't Call Yourself That

It hurts when I realize I am struggling
With my own thoughts
Like a wrestling match where
We fight with sheer mental strength
In who gets to choose what comes out
Of my mouth.

These days I am losing against
The obsessive and compulsive tendencies
Of my brain that is craving human connection
At the expense of moderation.

Those moments are where I seem to unlearn
Everything I have worked so hard in building
When it comes to human interactions
And getting to know one another.

Even my closest friends are put on the
Shelf of maybes, uncertains, and most likely
Find me utterly annoying and to be disposed of
With that fake smile and politeness that hide
their
True intentions of never talking to me again.

I know how irrational these thoughts sound
To someone who knows me and have witnessed
My cheerful face and easy conversation
Not realizing how underneath I was drowning
In the heavy waters of depression and
self-doubt.

"I KNOW IT WILL PASS" I yell to myself
As a part of me curls up into themselves
And cries on our bathroom floor.
"STOP YELLING AT YOURSELF," another
part
Shouts back with so much self-love and empathy
I still don't know how I deserved that fragment
of
My mind.

Waking up this morning was the first time
In weeks where my head didn't feel heavy
Carrying the apathy wrapped around my being
Which brought on waves of realization.

The acknowledgement of how often I used
Inebriation as a coping mechanism to feel,
Anything,
Other than deep despair and inner loathing.

With the clarity of mind that comes when
Somehow neurological connections have chosen
To function in a healthy and balanced way
I hold myself near and tell me it was okay.

I did what I needed to do when I couldn't
Think of anything else and with having all
The people I care about live so far away
I held on and clung to what little human
Interaction I could find, while juggling
The sincere fascination I have for new
Living creature and their beautifully
Diverse and uniquely functioning brain.

I'm trying to be honest about the reality
That I am neurodivergent without it
Having to be such a big deal like
How some fragments of myself
Seem to think it to be.

So let's make this an invitation to
Share about the diversity of how our
Brains can work and how sometimes
Things get a little off-kilter or as if
One is running on a hamster wheel
With no end in sight and from that
Perspective no wonder the words
Are fighting so hard to come out.

"Make it stop" is what they are probably
Trying to say.
But nothing comes out
Except what is socially acceptable.

Who knew words had a mind of their own.

Sitting In Water

There is something wonderful about
Sitting in water.
A little hot but not too much,
Just enough to be able to soak
Still, quietly, for as long
As needed.

Because I do need this,
Even though he doesn't understand.
He is lounging on the shaggy rug
Power napping while snoring,
Oblivious to the joys of
Sitting in water.

Eventually, worried that I might drown,
He pokes his head in,
Pushing back the curtain,
Watching me.

"What is so great about being naked
In a tub of cooling water?"
He seems to ask.
Instead, he wants a drink,
Gulping mouthfuls of my
Bath water.

I go back under,
Covering my ears
Hearing the makeshift waves
And the sounds of home
Through my underwater bubble.
This is my alone time.

She is too curious to not come looking,
At some point I open my eyes and pull myself up,
Seeing her peeking at me from the ledge,
Wondering what is so great about lying down
Almost fully covered in water.

I close my eyes again and soak in the warmth,
Knowing that it's my little secret and pleasure
To hide behind the shower curtain,
Neck deep in lukewarm water,
Just because.

I hear a noise,
Thinking it was my eldest,
I pull back the curtain to see,
Startling her in the process.

Poor darling,
She also does not understand
Where I came from,
Why I am still there,
And my choice to go back.

I pull the curtain closed again,
Telling them all,
"Just a little longer."

Even after I see his shadow
Pacing outside the tub,
Letting out a big sigh
And lying down on the rug,
I sit still.

Even after I see another little eye
Stare curiously in the gap
Wondering, most likely,
About my sanity,
I soak a little more.

Finally, after who knows how long,
I quickly wash myself,
Rince,
Dry,
And step out.

My dogs and cats look up at my naked body,
Unchanged,
Still not understanding
Why humans enjoy
Sitting in water.

I'll Try Harder

Can I come home to someone who is happy to
see me?
Instead of getting the cold shoulder for whatever
Triggered them that day at work,
Instead of needing to step up and support
A loved one who struggles every day to stay
alive
Due to their mental health issues.

Can I be the one who is cared for, just for a little
bit?
A small break of giving my support, my love,
My empathy, my time, my smiles, my
enthusiasm,
To everyone else,
Then go home to my beautiful furry babies that
also
Need so much from me.

Is it too much to ask to be the one to receive?

I'm sorry, I'll try harder.

I'll try harder to keep up at school even when
my mind

Makes me believe that life is hopeless and that no one
Cares if I fail or die or never reach out again
Which is hard to think otherwise when I am burnt out,
Missing weeks of school and having absolutely
No one check in on me.

I thought they wanted to be friends?
Or are we just friends when I am happy?

I'm sorry, I must not be trying hard enough.
I've been here for years,
Yet have no social circle.

No one asks me to make plans or invites me to
Anything.
It's not like I am waiting for everyone else to include me
In their lives.
I ask.
I ask them out for coffee,
For dog walks,
For playing videogames online,
For texting funny nonsense to each other.

And for all the enthusiastic nods of agreement,
No one follows through.
And the only common factor is me.

So I'm sorry, I must not be trying hard enough.
Maybe I don't understand the social norms,
Or I'm a little too quirky even for the local
weirdos.
Or not the right kind of weird.

I'm sorry I'll try harder to smile bigger,
To laugh louder, to create more colourful
Pieces of art, to not mention anything about my
Mental health.

I'll try harder to heal,
Meditate more,
Talk to my doctor more,
Go to therapy more often,
Take even more meds,
Eat even less sugar,
Be more chill.
If I keep trying, keep popping pills
That mute the worst of the bad thoughts
Then maybe I can be someone who's fun to be
around.

I don't want to sound whiny,
Even less sound self-pitiful or
Victimize myself when I am aware of the
Amount of privilege I have from the colour of
My skin and the amount of money in my
savings.

I'll try harder to live up to my privilege,
I'll be more grateful,
Take more walks outside,
Keep pushing myself to leave the
House because it's just anxiety and anxiety
Isn't that crippling if you tell yourself it isn't
because
Mental health is just about trying harder right,
Just think happy thoughts, and be more mindful
Always more mindfulness and empathy
Keep empathizing with people and listen and
support
And maybe if you just keep doing that then
maybe
People will want to hang out with me.

Nevermind dating,
Because of the lack of trust and the
hypersexualization
Of women's bodies, no matter what you identify
as
Your body is an object of lust and desire and if
you
Ever forget how much it is worth then that's
when you
Find yourself in a dark alleyway with a blocked
path ahead

Or a hangout with a friend who suddenly wants you to just
Drink a little more and hey it's all okay because we've known
Each other and just why are you so reserved because
Sex is someone everyone wants, right? Sex and penetration
And pleasing the male is what defines a successful relationship right
So if you don't want it and don't desire it and somehow want to be
Valued for your brain and amazing curiosity for life and what if you
Just want to feel like you can hug someone or lean on a person without
Getting groped or having a hand roam up a hem or down a shirt is that
Too much to ask?

I'm sorry, I'll try harder.
Maybe the four different pills I'm on and the therapy
I do and the plants that fill my house and the colour on my walls
And all the animals that live with me are not enough and I just need to
Try harder, right?

For some reason, my brain stays sad,
No matter what I do,
And I am so scared that it's been sad for so long
That it forgot how to be happy.

They throw words around to explain my mind
Like obsessive-compulsive disorder or
ADHD that comes with so much impulsivity
And creativity and so many thoughts that are
Wonderfully diverse and beautiful to see what
They come up with if you watch them go until
They get stuck on a dark thought and can't
Let go until it's all I can see.

But it's more than that because then I hear the
word
Major depression and general anxiety disorder,
Which I'm getting tired of hearing because I still
have
All these thoughts and my brain is still sad no
matter
How many pills they give me and how much
therapy
I do.

So how much harder do I have to try?
If I don't try at all I am sad,
If I give it my all I am sad,
If I try somewhere in the middle I am still sad.

So what is it?
Why is MY brain sad and not my neighbour's?
Why can't I celebrate the friends I have even
though
They live hours away and it took years of
trust-building
To get to where we are?

I'm sorry, I'll try harder.
What else can I do, right?

Hello Neighbour

I saw her through my screen door,
Just when I was about to take out the garbage,
I paused.
"What if she wants to talk?" I wondered,
A second's pause,
Wait…
What if I want to talk as well?
I caught myself
Thinking.

With everything happening around the world
Getting close to people is something I avoid
As someone who has social anxiety
Getting close to people is something I avoid,
Yet…

I remembered my family telling me I might be
Surprised,
At how slowly but surely this place could
become
My home,
My neighbourhood.

Don't get me wrong,
Moving at the start of a pandemic
Is definitely not the best way
To meet people.

And that's precisely why,
Instead of closing my front door,
And hiding behind it until my neighbour left,
I opened the door and called out:
"What a wonderful day we are having!"

With her young rambunctious puppy, and
perched on her walker
She looked up and smiled,
"Indeed it is," she answered.
And we talked, standing in the sunshine,
Those first glimpses of spring encouraging
Us to soak as many rays in before the
temperature
Dropped again.

As we talked,
A man stopped by in his car, saying hello to the
puppy
He had somehow nicknamed him Snowflake,
(I still don't know his real name)
And chatted a bit, blocking the road,
Before waving goodbye and heading back home.

I didn’t know him yet,
But I waved as well,
Because I am a neighbour now,
And we neighbours wave to each other,
As a community, in solidarity,
To remind each other we are not alone.

Finally, with her little puppy safely stowed away
Her walker’s basket, she said she should really
Be heading back
(three houses back, to be precise)
And dropping off my garbage,
I told her it could wait until my return and would
she mind
If I accompanied her home?

We slowly walked down the street together,
Sun shining down on us,
Her sharing about her husbands, cousins,
children,
How she lived all around and somehow ended
up here,
Blessing her little dog that was a Christmas
present from
Her family and the main reason that got her out
of bed
And walking outside this past year.

I talked about my cats and my studies,
And how the only people I hug now is my
elderly client
I see on the weekend.
We talked a little more,
And mutually extended the invitation to see each
other again
Maybe walk around the block next time,
Tiny puppy's paw permitting
(He had sprained it play-fighting, you see)

As I was leaving, she asked me my name.
I told her it was Gabby,
"Ahhhhh, I see. That's why you talk so much,"
she laughed.
I joined in on the joke and wished her a lovely
rest of the day,
Now heading to the post office down the street.

You see, I'm not perfect,
As I have an irrational fear of asking for people's name,
So I made a new friend,
Still nameless,
That reminded me why I love connection so much,
A person who gave me hope that maybe this could
Actually become my neighbourhood,
One wave at a time,
One walk around the block at a time,
One introduction
And well-intentioned desire to connect
At a time.

My Love

Yesterday, I was sad.
I told myself that maybe liquid courage would help me.
But, of course not.
It wasn't a case of reconfiguring one's nervous system back to ground zero.
It was a case of loneliness.
Existential loneliness was hitting me hard again,
Drowning me in its hold.
And I was mad at myself again.
Frustrated that I wasn't raised with a silver spoon in my mouth,
Confident in being loved and how to love.
I wasn't taught to love properly.
And I feel it, that Love, my Heart, outside of me,
Searching for a home.
I tell her:
"I'm right here! Aren't I enough?"
"HEY! Come back. I'm right here."
"We're a family, you and I,
Isn't that enough?"
My Heart turns to me, staring me down,
Knowing I know better than to ask,
Yet proceeding to answer:
"No, of course it's not enough."

Still, she comes back to me,
Holds me in her arms,
And lets me cry.
My Love is so strong.
She keeps trying, keeps picking me back up.
My Heart never gives up on me.
I see it in the way she looks at me,
Fierce determination in her gaze that reads:
"You are loveable and I shall find you your
chosen family,
I promise."
That's what keeps me going as well as makes me
cry at night,
That promise.
How long will my inner love, my heart,
Keep searching for me?
Wouldn't it be easier if we just kept to ourselves,
Turned all that love inwards?
My Heart looks at me with motherly gentleness
then,
Allowing me my pity party,
Proceeding to hold me close as I fall asleep
alone
Once more.
That's when she whispers to me,
When my dreams have carried my soul away
Into another adventure:
"You are destined for so much more.
You were born to help others,

To help so many people.
This pain is necessary.
One day you will understand."
My heart looks at me with so much love,
It's hard to imagine she feels all
This suffering as well.
"One day, it'll all make sense,"
She reiterates as she snuggles back into my chest,
Into the cavity that pumps blood through my veins,
Joining me in my dreams.

Feels

Do you remember the days when we'd put headphones in,
Cranked the music, and somehow,
The lyrics healed us,
Through all our teenage feels.

Everything felt so
Serious.

So I tried it again,
Every heartbreak,
I put in my headphones,
Cranked up the volume,
And let the music cry for me.

One of the things I looked forward to,
As a grown-up,
Is not having everything be so
Serious,
So,
End-of-the-world,
Life or death,
Kind of feels.

Somehow, I thought I'd grow into wisdom,
And knowing emotions were temporary.
What I didn't plan,
Was still having all those feelings, but
Also having wisdom.

No one ever mentioned the knives though,
All the wounds accumulated over years,
Still seeping blood,
With every trigger,
With every memory brought forward
By all the senses.

Younger, I wondered why adults didn't love
more,
Why they didn't love with all their heart,
Give into the sharing,
The connecting,
Being vulnerable with one another.

Then I got stabbed through the heart for the first
time,
And I understood why.
A broken heart here,
Shattered trust there,
Crumbled dreams on one side,
And the emptiness on the other.

I was told once that one has limitless love to give,
But how much can one bleed before it stops beating?
Or before it stops wanting to risk the pain
Of another missing part,
Atrophied,
Poisoned,
Lost?

Yet, I kept trying,
Accumulating the battle scars,
Finding my face wet from the tears,
And voice raw,
Asking again and again:
“Who are you?”
Asking myself who am I?

Every wound is a lesson,
Every scar leaves more room
For the next connection,
For a vulnerable leap into something new.
Be it friend, lover, stranger,
I will continue to love.
How sad would life be otherwise?

Blank Canvas

I've been gone for over a week,
Among familiar things, family,
And friends.

I've been able to be brave and hold it together,
Even though I only made one friend in my new city,
These past months.

I come back to where I used to live and within a day,
I see five friends,
We talk, laugh, share, exclaim, cry,
So openly.

I forgot what it was to have so many loved ones,
At a few minutes reach,
Where we can talk face-to-face.
I miss seeing people in person.

I miss knowing a friend is a phone call away.
These days, when I feel sad,
I stay home alone with my cats.

It’s only pathetic if I let it.
It’s only sad if I choose it to be.
I’m only lonely if I see it that way.

Because I’ve also been able to read again,
Do yoga,
Start learning how to dance,
I’m touching paint once more, canvas,
I have so many creative outlets.

I am resilient,
I am not afraid to cry or say that I am hurting,
And I am a fighter.

That doesn’t mean I don’t miss having friends around.
That doesn’t mean this isn’t hard,
To start from scratch,
All on my own.

But what if I choose to see it as a blank canvas,
Instead of an empty home?
I can paint it any colour,
And use any media,
Throw some glitter on top of it all,
While listening to really loud music one day,
And gentle piano the next.

This is my blank canvas;
I spent the first month staring at it blindly, numb.
I spent the second one crying, throwing anything on,
I'm spending the third one shaping the lines
Into something beautiful, new,
Allowing myself to be scared of what's to come,
And also excited.

It's been over a week,
Back with my family for early holidays,
My body can finally relax and is shutting down,
My eyes keep closing, finally feeling safe,
To curl up and cry, with no judgment.

"I'm excited!"
"I'm scared!"
"I'm lonely!"
"I'm thriving!"
"I don't know."
"I am trying."
" I'm still hurting."

"It's okay," says my friend.
"Thank you for sharing," says another.
"I empathize," says my buddy.
"Can I hug you?" asks my bro.

"Your canvas really looks like you," they all say.
Even I say it.
I haven't felt like myself in a while, so
This feels good.

Heading back home, hours away.
To a full house of cats,
To dancing and singing again,
To playing, creating, cooking again,
To being myself, a little bit more every day,
To my terrifying and exciting blank canvas.

Chronically What?

Sit straight,
Neck even straighter,
And when you eat
Don't eat too much,
Or too fast,
Too greasy or
Too crunchy,
Too spicy or
Too late at night.

Don't move right after you eat,
Explain to the children that if you do
You might throw up.
So it becomes my motto:
"Miss Gabby doesn't give piggybacks
After she eats or else she'll vomit
All over us."

At least the children simply
Look at me in a curious way.
That's just how miss Gabby is.
Piggybacks have a schedule.

Meanwhile, I am trying not to have
My food climb back up my throat
Into my mouth,
Burning a path along the way;
A reminder that things aren't
The same anymore.

Only a few weeks ago,
I thought it was the warning sign
That a migraine was on its way.
If only.

Instead,
I can now add acid reflux to the list of
Chronically what?

I have chronic generalized anxiety,
OCD, depression, ADHD, migraines,
And now acid reflux.

It is a journey of cautious list-making
Of what might be the reason or the trigger
That is keeping me home in bed today.

A journey of trying pills, a different
combination,
Adding a new one to manage the side effects
Of the first one, but then the other medications
React together so let's try another cocktail…

Trial and error,
Trial and error,
Trial and error,
With a smile.

I got to the point where my pharmacist would ask me
If it was really needed because all it felt like
Every time I came in I had a new prescription
To add to the long list of
"What will hopefully help."

Chronically what means that I miss work,
Missing work means that I need to hustle
A little harder to pay the bills.

It means I can't walk my dogs,
So I leave them outside in the beautiful
Backyard I created for them,
Hoping they understand that it's not
That I don't care,
But that even if I do care so much,
I can't get up and walk

Because the world spins
And nausea kicks in,
So I can't go to the park with them
With all the pain in my head

Pounding harder with the sun,
The heat, the noise,
The weather.

During these moments of
Chronically whatever,
The world has become such a
Minefield of overstimuli.

It means I lie in bed,
Inclined because actually lying down
Means everything comes back up,
But sitting too much means the
World starts spinning again.

And somehow,
Between the doctor's appointments
To ask if they can please try me on
Something else that might work,
Between changing my diet, practicing
Mindfulness, journaling,
Listening to my therapist tell me more
Ways that will help heal my mind,
I am trying to graduate from my third
Year of university and
Work full-time,

Because I'm a homeowner now,
And I have a family of rescues to

Care for,
And I am trying so hard to
Succeed at University which,
For most of my life was an
Unattainable dream because of my
Chronically whatever it was
At the time.

What does it mean to be
A human who has
Chronically what?

It means hoping your teachers understand
When you ask them for yet another extension
Because you spent the whole week just trying
Not to rip your head off from the pain.

It means getting impatient and frustrated
With the amount of powerlessness that comes
With your mind and body hurting for no
Apparent reason even though you went through
All the lists and made sure you slept enough,
Drank enough, ate well and regularly,
Talked about your feelings, let go of your
feelings,
Did nothing, Did something,
Took self-care time off for yourself.

It means the people on the outside don't
Understand when you snap at them,
Or don't answer your texts,
Or seem to disappear for days on end,
Because it isn't personal;
It's simply chronically whatever.

It doesn't matter.
Chronically what doesn't pay the bills,
Doesn't count as vacation,
Because most of that time spent home alone
Is not relaxing at all.

Chronically what means what?
It means phone calls and texts from coworkers
Asking you what's wrong,
Because you've missed so many days,
And how is that a valid excuse that you
"Don't feel well?"

Suck it up buttercup, right?
That is the society we live in.
The society where I tell my boss I feel like
Throwing up and they tell me how my coworker
Just lost someone last night and they're here
So can't I just suck it up and push through it?

Because what's wrong really, right?
Chronically what…

It's just me needing to get these thoughts out,
Process, share, explain, let go,
And now, hopefully,
Go get some amount of schoolwork done
So I don't fail.

Chronically what?
… Chronically trying, that is.

A Simple Hug

I need a hug,
A simple hug,
Something I never really thought of
As a privilege for some
And a daily ritual for others.

Hugs were one of the simple ways I said
"I love you" growing up.
I hugged everybody,
Feeling safe,
Sharing the love and the joy
Of connecting with others.

Then one day I turned into
What society would see
As a grown woman.
Suddenly hugs became unsafe
Sometimes undesirable from
Certain people with further intentions
Than just mutual and respectful
Appreciation of each other.

I don't know when I stopped giving hugs
Even to my closest friends.
Hugs felt dangerous,
Felt like giving people the opportunity
To touch me in a way I didn't want
And I couldn't know until the
Hug actually happened.

So I stopped.
But we are humans and we need touch
So what do you do when your needs
Are now in danger because suddenly
You became a sexualized being?

I remember thinking how much I
Wanted to hug the humans I loved the most
Yet at the back of my mind,
Body already tense,
This voice pleaded,
"Please don't take more than I offer,
Please don't cross my boundaries,
Please don't use me."

Then what?
How does one reacclimate into
Hug giving when a pandemic
Made sure we understood that
Proximity could mean death
And loneliness has plagued
So many individuals in the last
Years that I can't be sure that
A hug won't be a desperate desire
To touch flesh again.

With my closest friends living
The furthest away from me,
How do I ask for a hug?
How do I become human again?

A Little Faith

It is so easy to have little faith
In our neighbours,
The people crossing our path
Every day when we are
Out and about,
Society at large.

It is so much harder
To have faith
In others,
Strangers,
Family,
Friends,
Because what if we get hurt?

What if we make a faux-pas
And our mind fills with
Feelings of
Embarassment, confusion,
Betrayal, rejection?

What if we were too quick to
Judge
Not stopping to understand
How it feels to fill the other's
Shoes?

So our mind fills with
Anger, outrage, offense,
Powerlessness, sadness,
Shame, and avoidance.

Oh ye of a brain of your own
Will you have little faith
Or give trust a chance
And have faith in your
Kindred spirit?

I was sitting with my own
Mind believing
I was quite faithful to the world
While being confronted with the reality
That I let my emotions make me lose
Faith in others.

It was an argument, a misunderstanding
That was so easy to justify
With my self-righteous arguments
To myself.

It is so much easier to turn a cold
Shoulder to a person who offended us
Without asking ourselves why.

Why did they react that way?
Why did they feel the need to defend?
Why did I somehow feel like I was more
Deserving of an apology from them than
They from me?

Aren't we all human?
We make mistakes,
Hurt one another.
It's normal.

Yet the normal isn't normalized
As we lock our doors, turn our gaze,
Pull back our hand, look away,
And pretend that the person
Next to us is not as deserving
Of our level of privilege as
We are.

Who chooses to live in the street?
Who wakes up and says I want to be an addict today?
Who wants to live paycheck to paycheck?
Who deserves to be looked at with pity or disgust?

Who.

All those people are who's.
They are humans with needs, stories, emotions, family,
Friends, relationships, talents, qualities and faults,
Networks, connections, baggage,
So what makes us lose what little faith we have
In others while having no trouble giving it all
To ourselves?

"Have a little faith," they say in those big tall buildings,

With crosses on the walls, or holy books on their shelves
Without bothering to address how unequal we are all
Born into the world.

How does one have a little faith when
They can't even provide for their basic necessities?

Today was humbling for me,
A reminder that one needs to be present,
Listening, actively reaching out to life
With all the faith we have to stay open
To others,
Keep an open mind about other people's
Choices,
Be they in agreement with our own or not.
And if they're not, that is okay.

Having a little faith means knowing
That even though our life may look
So very different,
At the core of it, we all want what is
Best for one another.

That is what my faith looks like.

Pay It Forward

They say if you pay it forward,
It'll eventually come back full circle.
They say if you buy local,
You help others keep their jobs,
Which eventually helps everyone stay involved.
They say to think of others,
To give, to empathize, to volunteer.

.

It is said that if one smiles enough,
Then one's mind slowly starts to smile as well.
It is said to be nice, caring, considerate,
To make friends.
It is said that if one loves their job,
They will not have to work a day in their life.

.

I was told many things growing up,
I learned some by experience,
I've read about others,
I've observed, dabbled a little here and there,
I have been going and still go
To therapy.

.

I have cats,
Who protect from ghosts and spirits,
And who teach me that love
Has its ups and downs,
But healthy love stays.

.

Trauma has a way to twist
Distort
Break any casual and normal moment.
When one passes as a functioning
Human being,
It can be hard to say:
"I have trauma."
It can be harder,
After being triggered,
To explain the "why" behind such
Irrational behaviour.

.

Sometimes words aren't enough.
Sometimes trauma doesn't mean a thing
To someone dealing with their own issues.
Sometimes things break,
And it's unfortunate.

.

It's not always about the giving,
The empathizing, considering,
The kind thoughts, the handwritten letters,
It's not about caring at all.
Sometimes it's about who we choose
To care about.
Sometimes the hardest lesson
Is to learn to stop caring
For the wrong people.

.

The longer one lives,
The more chances one has to love.
Some see it as accumulating broken hearts,
While others find it a collection of meaningful meetings.
It depends
On so many things.

.

Some days my brain chemistry makes me think
Sad thoughts.
Dead thoughts.
Untrue thoughts.

.

Some days pure joy fills my heart
And reminds me that life is good,
That I am grateful to be alive,
To have a roof over my head,
To have food on the table,
To be going to school.
To have gone to school,
Grateful for cats,
Plants,
Rainbows,
And a home.

.

Some days it's a mix:
There is bliss intermingled with
Loneliness.
Because there is no one to share it with.

.

I don't need someone
But I am human.
And we are social creatures.
Connection is a real thing,
Some days I feel it more than others.
Tears remind me I care,
And hugs as well.

.

I share singing to connect,
I show my paintings to connect,
I model my cats to connect,
I encourage local businesses to connect,
I ask for mutual honesty to connect.
I do so much to connect,
Yet often still feel so lonely.

.

Maybe one day I can share a meal again,
With lovers,
Friends,
Family,
Kindred souls who'll stay nearby,
Look me in the eyes, and say:
"Hey, I get it."

.

One day.
Someone will pay it forward as well.

If You Take Away The Sound

I put on my headphones and headed outside,
Tuned into the song playing on repeat,
Telling me to look around and see,
While losing connection to the sounds around
me.

She was walking by my side,
Yet I couldn't hear her,
As she explored the streets one by one,
A slight pull here and a tug there,
Showing me where to go.

I couldn't hear you anymore,
Couldn't hear the voices asking me
How I was or what I was up to,
Couldn't hear the silence of home,
And the echo of dust motes.

Walking, focusing on one foot in front
Of the other, the feel of the gravel
Underneath my sole,
The change in terrain as we headed for the
Schoolground where a couple was snuggling
Into each other.

I couldn't hear them, the sounds of their bodies
Or voices exchanging what I assume would be
Sweet words and as I looked up he caught my
eye
Lips moving but with no sound;
What an odd sensation.

Taking off the headphones I apologized
For my intentional temporary deafness
Until I realized all they wanted was the time
So I told them 9 o'clock.

I was floating, in the repetition
And the familiarity of words so often
Heard and sung.
I felt safe, on a cloud of quietness
Although my ears were full of music.

There was no city around me,
Nor pedestrians walking by,
No neighbours chatting,
Or argumentative squirrels.

There was only me,
And my dog,
And one foot in front of the other;
Enjoying the small pleasures of life.

New Home Alone

Sometimes, all you have to do is

Sit in your car and cry,
To get a break from being needed
By those puppy dog eyes
Without having to explain why
Mom is too tired for a walk
Or why she sits on the floor a lot
Staring at a screen.

Sometimes, the car can be like
A bubble where people can't reach you
And you are sheltered from prying eyes.

Sometimes, your body gets so tired
Of being alone and having no one to call
Because all your friends live far away
And this new town doesn't yet feel like
Home, and what is home anyway?
When there is only yourself to wish
Good night to and lie beside of one's self
In bed.

I am tired. Exhausted. And with so little
Spoons left that I had to call into work
And ask for the weekend off, crying over
The phone because my job is to care for
Other people when right now I can barely
Take care of myself.

So, can you give me a break?
Remind me I am loved, squeeze me into
A tight hug until all of the pressure in my
Mind fades away and I am left bare,
A fresh canvas to start the week on
And maybe my depression can give me
A break as well.

Books

Wrap me in your arms and
Weave stories out of thin air
With wisps of imagination and
A sprinkle of disbelief.

Remind me how there is more
Than an alarm clock ringing and
A drive down the highway to
Pay the bills and keep a roof over my head.

Tell my heart how there is beauty in the
Mundane and potential for greatness
In every creature walking down the sidewalk
No matter its shape or size.

Erase the doubts that reside
Deep inside my soul that magic
Is dead even though it has survived history
And has felt the hand of faith.

Stack piles and piles of pages
One on top of the other and fill
Them with so many letters strewn
Together to create a life out of nothing.

Help me feel emotions I would never feel
Without your gentle and sometimes harsh
Reminders that there are more stories out there
Than I will ever have time to discover.

Fill hours of a clock with lifespans
And minutes of its hands with universes
All the more unique and real than the other
While reminding me to open my eyes.

Hold me tight as I fall into despair
Leaving years of tears in my wake
And sheer wonder as to how a human
Can ever feel anything again.

Reassure my mind when it is sick
And dark clouds take over every space
In this cavity that contains all the worlds
And experiences that I call my own.

Remember me when I am alone
And have lost the way to my own
Adventure because society enjoys
Crushing dreams with piles of paperwork.

Connect us in our quest for the shadows
And shapes taking form all around us
When we dare to look for the magic
That is and has always been alive.

Allow me to heal between your pages
Even when you aren't at all in the mood to talk
But have the graciousness to say nothing
When I crinkle your paper with my tears.

And never stop making people laugh
Together or on their own
From a chuckle to an uncontrollable
Belly holding, painful expulsion of joy.

Make It Stop

The nausea
Of too many sleepless nights
And so many overflowing feelings
That fill my stomach
Asking me to make it stop.

So I write,
Leaving space for the feelings
To form on paper,
Allowing my emotions
The voice to let me know
What's on our mind.

I feel a fog in my brain
And my insides are churning
While my mind decides it
Will not and cannot
Focus on anything.

... Great.

I feel the tug of academia
Asking me why I haven't been
Working on that assignment due

Next week worth most of my grade.
Grades.

"What is so important about numbers"
My nausea seems to ask me,
"When you have emotions waiting to be told?"
I wonder.
"Why waste time on letters," it continues,
"When you can weave stories out of feelings?"
I grow sad.
Why indeed...

I am reminded of how little I like sitting at a desk
Typing away my life for projects that will lead to Nowhere,
And remember how growing up,
I believed I would become a painter,
And live in a cabin in the woods.

Where did my art go?
When did everything around me become so Sterile?
How long have I been paper-pushing
While forgetting the voices of the world?
I feel hollow.

My headache increases,
Pressure building,
Nausea pushing inside my throat
As ocean waves crash
Into high walls built
Around my heart.

When did I stop hearing the voices?
Where have all the colours gone?
And the music?
Can I find them in a textbook?
And if not, what does that mean about me?

Where do I go from here?

What Progress Really Looks Like

It started in my throat as my breath caught,
It felt like someone slowly wrapping both their hands around
My neck and squeezing.
"Let me breathe," my lungs seemed to ask those imaginary hands.
I remember those hands,
Who they belong to.

Anxiety.

It had been a while since I felt it this way;
It has a way of showing up in such diverse forms,
You'd think I'd be in awe of their skills if it wasn't
For the havoc it wreaked upon my life.

I noticed it as if from far away,
Almost like it was happening to somebody else.
It felt like my brain looking down and noticing
How my heart seemed to be struggling to
Release the grip of those imaginary hands upon
My imaginary throat.

So much imagination,
Yet it felt so real.
So, as my brain seemed to be looking from above,
I watched myself struggle to breathe.

This is progress, the not simply choking up the
Anxiety and drowning from swallowing
Mouthfuls and mouthfuls of anxious thoughts,
Salty waves of pure worry, insecure extrapolations
About the overwhelming and endless ocean of
Insurmountable tasks and goals to accomplish.

This progress feels so good,
To see the potential of drowning,
But focusing on every single inhalation.
The sensation of my lungs filling,
Chest rising, ribs expanding,
Then slowly exhaling,
Hearing the sound of the air leaving my body,
Until I start all over again,
Aware,
Present,
In the moment.

I could feel the anxiety wanting to drive out
All trace of reasonable thinking and awareness,
Rushing in to lose all sense of rationality,
Building momentum with the compulsion of release,
On the feeling of pressure against my mind,
Pushing at my scalp, demanding an escape.

I felt the urge and continued to focus on breathing,
While also starting to make sugar cookies;
The compulsion,
It was there,
If only faint.

I remember how bad it used to be,
How it would force me to swallow bowls full of
Raw sugary dough, packs of cookies, chocolate bars
By the dozen,
So much food that made the pressure go away,
At least for the moment.

I don't remember the last time I felt that compulsion,
Never like the days of my eating disorders,
Not like those times where I lost control so
completely
I would wake up in a park rummaging through a
garbage can
Looking for food.
Not that bad.

But it was there, that need, that promise of release,
If only I ate all those cookies.
I kept breathing, calmly,
Aware that I was anxious,
Conscious that my compulsion to eat
Was a cry for help,
A distraction from the pain underneath.

My body was telling me it was hurting,
Somewhere.
My mind was asking me to make it stop hurting,
The idea of looking at those feelings,
Turning my attention towards those emotions,
Increased the urge to bake and consume,
A sure sign that what my anxiety didn't want me looking at,
Was exactly where I had to turn my attention.

This is what progress looks like.
It isn't clean or magical.
It doesn't suddenly mean I can perfectly manage my mood swings,
Or avoid all triggers,
Or diffuse my irrational meltdowns.

It simply means I am a little more aware than I used to be,
I can stay present a little longer on the edge of the battlefield
In my mind where my wild, wounded, triggered, cornered,
Animal of a traumatized state is fighting to survive.

I still get pulled in and completely engulfed by the beast at times,
But mostly I see it scared and alone, lost and confused,
And I can be my own gentle saviour,
Coaxing it back to safety and trust,
Awareness and understanding.

Mostly, I am not just the wounded wild one anymore.

That is what progress really looks like.
Now, sitting, belly full of only a few cookies instead of the whole batch,
Tired and questioning instead of compulsive and confused,
Aware and breathing slowly instead of losing connection with my body
And destroying any sense of stability.

The progress is that I am still present right now,
I could see what was happening and influence its outcome,
I managed to stay present and not lose connection with my mind
Or my body.

And that feels amazing.

Just A Little Girl

I was just a little girl,
For most of our time together,
Just a little girl,
Inside a grown woman's body.

It started off so well,
With kind words, gentle looks,
Our bodies couldn't get enough,
Time seemed to have stopped for us.

Then came a little lie,
That twisted into another one,
Telling me it wasn't what you said,
Being told it was all in my head.

We loved each other though,
So I gave it a shot,
"We're getting the problems out early,"
You told me, yet it never stopped.
I asked you what you wanted,
The answer kept being "I don't know."
I told you what I wanted,
It didn't match,
So I asked you to let me go.

I was blamed for not trying,
Blamed for giving up,
Shamed for having different dreams,
And put down every time I stood up.
You loved me though,
Is what you kept saying,
Promising to try harder,
Promising there'll be changes.

Slowly the woman died inside of me,
And the little girl came out,
Asking what she did wrong this time,
Smiling, pleasing, smoothing things out.
The little girl kept crying,
But no one saw her tears,
The little girl kept speaking,
But not a word could anyone hear.

Because he loved her he said,
And the problem was her.
Because she was told if she tried harder,
Then things would get better.
So she started bleeding,
From this wound inside her chest,
Bleeding from the heart,
Onto the floor, onto the walls,
Poisoning her dreams and all.

She lost sight of herself,
With all the blood covering her face,
Clogging up her throat,
Nothing ever felt safe.
But no one saw the blood,
Only saw the smiles,
She started throwing up all over,
Words here, screaming there,
So much blood and pain everywhere.

She kept asking if she was crazy,
If anyone else saw it everywhere.
All of these emotions,
Poured out of her wounds,
Onto unwary humans,
Who fled at the gruesome sight.
With so many fleeing,
She was left more alone,
With him saying he loved her,
And that this was her home.

If only she fit into this box,
And kept her feelings down,
If only she smiled more, was more fun,
He'd get better and work something out.

You have to try harder,
Was all the little girl heard,
These tears are hurting people,

Just shut up and play, learn.

Learn and learn she did do,
Until she could learn no more,
Still she wasn't happy,
And the little girl swore.

Out came the anger,
Of never being heard,
Out came her frustrations,
Yelling, burning bridges,
Letting out all the words.

For somewhere deep inside,
The adult found the light,
Crept up to the surface,
And saw such suffering and fright.

She took the girl by the hand,
Shut out all that he had said,
Reminded the girl of what love is,
How good, kind and wonderful it was.

They took all their belongings,
Left the town they loved behind,
Found a job, applied to school,
And made it work out.

The wounds are still healing,
From the island she called home,
From a boy who had loved her,
And the family that was found.

All of this is behind her,
As she sits in her colourful little house,
Surrounded by cats, plants and laughter,
With a family of one.

At times she gets lonely,
And the little girl starts to cry,
For how could they have loved her,
While killing her inside.

Those times the adult girl,
Takes the littler one and says
That all her feelings are valid,
That she is seen, she isn't dead.

The adult holds the child closer,
Reminding her of her own strengths,
Embracing her emotions,
For her words and thoughts, she thanks.

Some lessons leave one hurting,
With scars blistered up and red,
Months and years continue aching,
From the memories in my head.

So I am trying to let go now,
And learn what healthy love is,
Reminding me of how I walked away,
For my dreams and so I could live.

When the aches come back,
And I start to doubt myself,
I think of my little girl,
Or her strength, resilience, and courage
To keep exploring the world

I Take It Back

I take it back,

The words, the feelings, the expressions,
Shown on my face,
I take it back,
The silence, the dreams, the wishes,
Of being understood.

.

I take back the possibility that you are good,
The opportunity for vulnerability,
And the space for growth and change.

.

I take back the giddiness, the tears,
The shared words between friends.
I take back how much, or how little,
Or how I don't want to know if I care.

.

I take back the awareness, the empathy,
The wisdom to know the unrealistic
expectations,
Of perfection, of telepathy, and eternity.

.

Oh how I take back the risk,
And the stories I made up in my head.

How angry I am at Hollywood for making me
believe,
This is what is considered normal and desired.
.
I take back my daydreams,
I take back my angst,
I take back my thoughts of you.
.
If only I could take myself back to the
beginning,
Maybe then my path would lead me to see,
How life isn't about taking back and regrets,
But about dreams, trials, and believing in me.

Those Dark Clouds Never Really Leave

I'm struggling to find the words,
That will let the tears come out,
And maybe help lift these clouds,
That have chosen to keep me company
for the weekend.

It reminds me of the years
When they were the only
Friends I had.
Always somewhere close enough,
That I knew I was never truly alone.

I told myself that if I put on music loud enough,
It would finally rain,
And I'd see the sun,
By morning.

But my tears aren't falling,
They're hovering,
Waiting,
For what?

So I keep the music on repeat,
Try putting it a little louder,
And I start to think of doing something else,
Because clearly nothing is coming out.

That's when the tears come up,
Right on the edge of my eyes,
"Don't leave," they seem to say,
"We have something to tell you,"
They insist.

I am tired of my body filling my mind
With dark clouds,
To let me know of an off-kilter
Element in my life,
Because I don't know
What they're trying to say.

I cried in my car today,
Reaching out to a friend,
Telling them how bad the thoughts were,
Droning on about how alone I am and
How little my friend actually cared.

I told them I fought the thoughts,
Repeating to myself how it wasn't true,
Reminding my mind of the simple fact
That I am lovable.

Do you know how it feels,
When your brain decides to stop
Any positive thoughts?
You wake up and the joy is dead.
The thought of life holds no meaning.

"Oh," I'd tell myself on those occasions,
"It's that time again."
That time when I lose all reason to live
While simultaneously knowing it's not true.

Deep down inside, I know it isn't real,
But my mind is so good at making it seem
Otherwise.

The sadness fills me, slowly,
Intentionally,
Whispering in my ear...
"You know the drill," it says,
"So why are you still surprised?"

"Ha, wait," it laughs,
"You can't be surprised because I took
All of that away from you
And left only the void."

So I start crying again,
Thinking things were going so well,
Believing that maybe I was healed,
Maybe the dark clouds really had left
For good.

Is that really possible?

The struggle between intrusive thoughts
Is so strong.
A tug-of-war telling me no one would care
If I disappeared.

And the knowledge, so so far way,
But still there,
That I am loved by so many.

"If you are, then why are you alone here?"
It responds.
"Every
Single
Day,
Why doesn't anyone come knocking?"
It mocks me.
"Is that how people show their love,
By leaving you alone?"
It insists.

The voice is so good at twisting words
Into something they're not.
I almost threw away my relationship
With my friend this weekend,
Because it was telling me
How none of it was real,
And I almost believed it.

I fought so hard to remind my mind
That I have friends,
That people care,
That this feeling will pass.

Isn't this just my time of the month?
Maybe it's the shock of coming home
After weeks away,
And maybe the pandemic is finally
Getting to me.

Deep down inside though,
A part of me wonders if
This is just my normal.
Maybe I'm not meant to
Feel happiness on a daily basis.

Maybe depression is supposed to be
One of those life-long friends,
That always seems to find their
Way back no matter time or place.

I cried,
Finally,
I wrote down my fears,
The darkness in my head,
And I feel its hold loosen,
I can breathe again.
Relief.

I mostly feel relief
From the noose in my brain
Losing some of its hold.

It doesn't solve anything,
But maybe I can get some of my
School work done.
Maybe I can do something,
Just a little.

And maybe tomorrow morning
It will simply feel as if I had
Woken up from a really bad dream.

Maybe.

Cheesy

Living in the middle of the woods,
All by myself,
I get lonely.

As much as I enjoy the company of my cats,
Even though I am grateful for my home
And the colors on my walls,
I am lonely.

So on those days where it feels a little heavier,
Give me cheesy.
When I start getting overwhelmed,
Assignments piling up,
On top of chores and the responsibilities
Of running a house on my own,
Give me cheesy.

Cheesy gives me a break from
The stress inside my head,
The voices telling me romance is dead,
From the fighting, mental health issues,
Allowing space to breathe.

Cheesy gives me hope that things will turn out fine,
That fights, and break-ups, and relationships,
Somehow always find a way back to being okay.
That families and friends are there and have your back,
That single can be cool if it's on the big screen
And you have the right make-up on
With a matching outfit.

Now, don't get me wrong,
Even though I am a tomboy,
Believe in anarchist relationships
And the expression of our true selves
No matter societal standards,
I love myself a cheesy movie.

Sometimes I need to spend a few hours
Immersed in a world where there is a soundtrack
To every emotion,
A story that shows you the happy ending
And the illusion that lame is another form of cool.

Every few weeks,
My emotions need an external purge
And a deep cleaning of my mental hard drive.
Don't give me due dates and appointments,
Don't remind me of deadlines and my to-do list.

Just let me live,
Vicariously,
Emotionally,
Optimistically,
Someone else's life with their problems
That somehow all fall into place.

If I watch it long enough,
The anxiety goes away,
My fatigue slowly disappears,
And my cup is refilled.

If I give myself a break from the need-to's
For a little bit of my want-to's,
I am reminded of how life is a balance
Of useful and frivolous moments
Intertwined into an interesting story
That is my own.

For those harder days,
I need me some cheesy.

www.ingramcontent.com/pod-product-compliance
Lightning Source LLC
Chambersburg PA
CBHW051733130826
49812CB00033B/849
9789395784085